SHOTS FIRED!

HOW TO WRITE COPY THAT PIERCES HEARTS

(And Opens Wallets)

APRYL BEVERLY

Disclaimer: The information contained herein is general in nature and for informative purposes only. It is based on the author's personal experience. The author assumes no responsibility whatsoever, under any circumstances, for any actions taken as a result of the information contained herein.

Some names and identifying details have been changed to protect the privacy of my clients and colleagues.

ISBN: 1523497805
ISBN-13: 978-1523497805

DEDICATION

To my "everythings," Bakari and Alston Beverly, I love you two so much – thanks for being my WHY. I thank God each and every day for blessing me with you.

CONTENTS

ACKNOWLEDGMENTS

First and foremost I praise God for blessing me with the gift of words and the grace to wake up every day and do what I love.

Thank you to my mom, Mary Mosby, who always pushed me to follow my passion (as long as it involved college and being an independent woman).

To my dad, Alfonza Steadman, who taught me things I never knew I needed to know but am so glad you took the time to teach me.

To my brother, Alfonzo Steadman, Jr., for always believing in me. You call me your "little big sister," but you've been the one protecting me, big bro.

To my awesome family and friends, naming each of you would require every page in this book and "ain't nobody got time for that." Know that I truly thank you for being my prayer warriors and my champions – your faith encourages me.

To my wonderful crew of "biz buddies," writers, editors, proofreaders and designers who redefine the word "competitors," I appreciate all that you do to support me and the BAAB Writing and Marketing Services dream.

And last but not least, this book wouldn't be nearly as helpful without the amazing solo entrepreneurs, CEOs, business owners, marketing executives, sales directors and many others who hire me to write copy that makes them money. I appreciate you and am forever grateful for your support.

INTRODUCTION

I received a ton of criticism for referencing the word "shots" in the title and throughout this book. They say it implies violence and with mass shootings happening way too much in the United States and around the world, there's no need to reference guns of any sort in a book about copywriting. While I understand their arguments, I don't whole-heartedly agree with their perspective of the word. As you'll see in this book, words have as much power as you, the writer, give them. And how people react to your words is a direct correlation to the power you give them.

This will all make much more sense as you dive into the book, but for now, just know that words have power. They can move you from bawling your eyes out to trembling with excitement to bursting into a rage and hurling a shoe across the room. The emotional triggers of certain words are evident in great novels, movies and music, but the power of words leaps far beyond storytelling

When you write emails, sales pages and website copy that make people feel something, you're much more likely to get them to do something: Invest in your service. Download your e-book. Register for your webinar. So, you're probably wondering . . . how?

The Internet is full of folks who can jot down a great idea or two, but to make those ideas pierce the heart of the reader, tugging and pulling at their emotions until they do exactly what you want, now, that's a superstar skill. The good news is, when you have the right tools and understand the magical formula of crafting spine-tingling sentences, this skill can be yours.

Skilled copywriters infuse their sales copy with carefully-selected, highly emotional words that draw the reader into their text and persuade them to take action. Granted, that's not all we do. Storytelling is a big part of it too.

Knowing all the tricks of the trade can take years to master. Heck, I've been in the copywriting game for 15-plus years and am still uncovering new ways to leverage the power of words! However, you can learn enough to craft your very own persuasive website copy, emails and sales pages so you won't need to hire an expensive copywriter. And in this book, that's exactly what I'm going to teach you to do.

So give me your hand and follow me through the wonderful world of copywriting. By the end of this book, you'll know my proven process for writing persuasive copy; and when you apply what I teach, you'll move from a beginner copywriter to a persuasive copywriting expert in no time.

HOW TO USE THIS BOOK

I shopped around the idea of comparing persuasive writing to "Copy Shots" in a few social media groups and was met with a great deal of opposition. Some folks said, "Go for it, Apryl," while others said using the word "shot" was in poor taste. It really got me thinking about the word and how it affects people. How it sparked nearly 100 comments from strangers in social media groups who know nothing about me or my hustle as a copywriter. Because of the passion I saw in each comment, I knew Copy Shots had to be the title of each chapter in this book.

Now, I've never been shot myself, but I know people who have, and my heart hurts for those who are victims of gun violence whether I know them or not. But beyond the act of violence, the word "shot" carries many meanings and touches people in different ways. Let's move outside the negativity of the word and think about the adrenaline rush a basketball player gets when he scores the game-winning "shot." And how about the joy people feel when they're standing at a Starbucks counter waiting to get their mocha latte with a "shot" of caramel.

Do you see how I completely flipped the power and energy of the word "shot" and made you feel a new emotion with each sentence? When I mentioned gun violence, you probably felt disgusted and sad. When I spoke about the winning shot, you cheered on the player, and when I talked about the shot of caramel, your tummy did a backflip.

The beauty of persuasive writing is that you, as the writer, have the power to tap into certain emotions to propel your reader into action. And that's what you'll learn to do in this book. Choose words and give them the power they need to get your reader to do what you want – buy your service, register for your webinar, or subscribe to your email list. Pierce their hearts because when you do, you're well on your way to getting them to open their wallets.

***

You'll get the most out of this book if you follow each of the five Copy Shots and if you complete each chapter's recommended exercises. Allow yourself 2 to 4 hours for each chapter. This gives you time to watch the mentioned videos, read the text (in depth and for a refresher) and immediately apply what you learn as you write your own persuasive copy.

Depending on the length of your sales page, Copy Shot #4 may take you a little longer.

Use this book to write great content for sales and opt-in pages. Apply the principles to write new website copy or to glam up an existing website. Use what I teach to turn your email subscribers into buyers. Bottom line: Once you understand the core principles of persuasive writing, you'll have the power to bang out words that sell virtually anything.

A 5-Day Plan

In a hurry to write your very own persuasive copy? Read one Copy Shot and do that chapter's included exercise all in a few hours of one day. This way, in 5 days, you could have a persuasive sales page or other piece of copy ready to wow your target client.

A 5-Week Plan

For those of you who like to savor the product, read a Copy Shot at the beginning of the week, do the corresponding exercise, and then let it simmer for a few days. Then go back and see if you have anything to add to your exercise. If you follow this plan, it will take you 5 weeks to write your sales page or other piece of persuasive copy.

Here is an overview of the 5 Copy Shots

Copy Shot #1: Why Writing for Everybody Ain't Working

The biggest mistake even professional writers make is writing for too many people. Your sales copy will be more persuasive if you focus on having a conversation with that one special person. This Copy Shot helps you write in a way that personalizes your message.

Copy Shot #2: I Got 99 Problems, Can You Solve One?

Be honest … have you ever taken the time to write a comprehensive list of all the facts and feelings that can persuade your reader to smack the buy button? This Copy Shot helps you get everything on paper so you don't miss any important "hooks" in propelling your readers into action.

Copy Shot #3: An Indecent Proposal

Like the popular 1993 film, Indecent Proposal, persuasive writing is about finding out people's weaknesses and using them to position your best offer. If you're not familiar with the movie, I'll explain later. For now, just know that inside this Copy Shot you'll discover how to craft your offer – the most essential part of your sales page. You'll also find out the ultimate secret to persuasive writing.

Copy Shot #4: The B.O.S.S. Sales Page Map

Now that you know how to position your offer, it's time to write the rest of your sales page. Here I'm going to reveal the structure I use to write sales pages that make my clients heaps of moolah. Remember, you can use these techniques to write website copy, send emails to your subscriber list and to craft virtually any other type of persuasive copy. I'm guiding you through the steps of writing a sales page because I want to make sure that while reading this book you are getting the necessary information you need to write copy that sells.

Copy Shot #5: You Ain't Done … Yet

I always tell clients to first write from heart to page. I do this because your brain can often get in the way of truly amazing copy. You start to think about sounding smart. Then you don't want to piss off anyone. And then you don't want to be too pushy. By the time you consider all these limiting thoughts, you've created a completely useless and watered down piece of copy. In Copy Shot #5, you'll discover simple tricks to transform that "raw" piece of copy into toe-curling sentences that capture the hearts, minds and pockets of your ideal clients.

***

A word of warning: You invested in this book, so please don't let it sit and collect dust. Learn and implement the lessons as you go. Write your own persuasive sales page as you read.

To help you craft persuasive copy like the BOSS I know you are, go ahead and download your FREE action sheets here:

www.baab.biz/FREEActionSheets.

Imagine having a six-figure copywriter sitting on your shoulder telling you exactly what to type to make your copy more persuasive. Sounds fabulous, right? Well, grab your action sheets and let's do this.

Download them now => www.baab.biz/FREEActionSheets.

One last thing – have fun! Now, say "cha-ching," and let's get started!

Copy Shot #1

WHY WRITING FOR "EVERYBODY" DOESN'T WORK

"I've learned that people will forget what you said, people will forget what you did, but people will never forget how you made them feel." — Maya Angelou

The biggest mistake solo entrepreneurs make is trying to write one heart-piercing, life-changing and business-booming message for too many folks at once. It makes the message wishy-washy, watered down and downright ineffective. By trying to talk to a crowd, you end up having a conversation with nobody at all.

Let me lay it out for you.

A few years back, "Vanessa" emailed me about writing a sales page for her. She's a local website designer who wanted to sell her services on the Internet. Here's how our first conversation went:

> **Me:** *"So who's your ideal client – what kinds of people do you love working with?"*
>
> **Vanessa:** *"Hmm, I'd say everybody who sells stuff. Every business needs a website designer, so I don't want to set a specific audience. Seems like that would limit the amount of money I can make."*
>
> **Me:** *"Funny you say that, Vanessa, because by NOT identifying your ideal client, you're limiting the amount of money you can make in your business."*

Believe it or not, a ton of solo entrepreneurs think just like Vanessa. They think by picking one specific reader to write to that they're excluding everybody else. When you write like you're engaged in a one-on-one conversation, you actually engage more people who face similar problems as your ideal client.

You think I'm pulling your leg, don't you?

Take, as an example, "Alissa." She's a website designer I came across early in my quest to write copy for solo service providers. I'd been working with corporate clients and was super excited to "de-corporatize" my website so solo entrepreneurs would know I can write for them too. And Alissa was just the girl to help me do that (or so I thought).

Anyway, she agreed to Skype with me and for the first 15 minutes of the call, I rambled on and on about all the changes I wanted on my site.

When I took a pause to breathe, Alissa said something that washed away all my excitement:

"I don't think I'm going to be able to help you," she said. I was shocked. Was it something I'd said? Was I not clear enough about what I wanted? Did she think I was a big dreamer with no cash? And then I got pissed off. How could she turn me away? Doesn't she need clients to pay her bills?

That was about 3 years ago and, after finally getting over my hurt feelings, I now know why Alissa told me to "kick rocks."

Hearing about my project didn't make her heart sparkle and her spine tingle. She didn't visualize herself laid-back, sipping margaritas on a sandy beach in the Bahamas after working with me. Alissa didn't see me as her dream client, so she cut me loose. Having worked with hundreds of solo entrepreneurs over the past few years, I understand that "all money ain't good money."

Sure, you can work for every Julie, Dave and Vanessa who comes your way. That's certainly your choice, but trust me, at some point, working with clients who don't make your own heart sparkle is going to wear you out. Because when you spend time slaving away on projects for clients like that, you waste time and miss out on attracting the people who would make you do the happy dance every morning when you jump out of bed.

My best advice to avoid killing your entrepreneurial vibe is to find out what type of clients you love and do great work for them. I promise, it's one of the easiest ways to grow a business ever invented.

Another big mistake I see solo entrepreneurs make is writing what you, as the service provider, like to write rather than what your client wants to read. This mistake is sometimes even made by professional writers because it's so hard to think like your reader.

If you want to persuade your prospect to buy something, you need to address his or her needs, hopes and desires. You need to crawl inside the head of your reader to gain her interest, to push her to read on, and to get her to smack the buy button. The most critical step you can take to make your writing more persuasive is changing your perspective and writing for your potential client instead of for yourself. This Copy Shot reveals everything you need to know to do exactly that. You'll discover:

- Why you should write for just one "dreamy" client
- How to describe your dreamy client to increase the effectiveness of your sales page
- How to uncover more about your dreamy client

At the end of this chapter, you'll be able to create your very own description of the perfect client for your business.

Why should you write to one special person?

Every marketing class you've ever taken talks about identifying your target audience. So shouldn't what you write for your business address everybody in your audience at the same time? Nope, and here's why:

A target audience is a faceless crowd. Writing to a group of people makes you sound as if you're lecturing. Folks don't like to feel like they're sitting in one of the 200 seats in a lecture hall. They prefer to read something that speaks directly to them. Describing and visualizing that one ideal client makes your writing more vivid and personal. It doesn't mean that you never attract anyone else to work with you. It means that whoever closely matches your description of the perfect client feels that your words are written divinely for her. And that gets her excited and engaged.

Imagine you need to write a sales page for your brand-new business coaching service, I Coach U (ICU). You offer private coaching sessions to help clients put systems in place to make their first $500 per week. This is huge because a lot of the new entrepreneurs you meet are still struggling to make their first $1.

You identify a services-based entrepreneur looking to build her business online as the perfect client for ICU's new coaching service. Let's call her "Brittany." Now, Brittany is what you might call a serial course taker. She's invested a ton of money in online courses and still hasn't landed her first paying client yet. She's a working mom with two children aged 5 and 7. Her corporate job drains the life out of her. She wants the freedom of entrepreneurship, but hasn't been able to make any money doing what she loves.

Brittany doesn't want to spend a lot of time going through yet another course. She's been burned by fluff, no-substance courses in the past. This time she expects to invest in a service that tells her not only what to do, but also how to do it so she can finally make enough money to quit her day job and be the entrepreneur of her dreams. She's not concerned about the coach's social media fame or how much money ICU has made. She only cares about working with someone who can help her make at least $500 a week to replace her corporate job income.

This short description of Brittany and her hopes and aspirations helps you to write a sales page for ICU. While as the service provider, you may be proud of your own personal successes and achievements, you don't need to highlight them here because Brittany doesn't care about all that.

So even though ICU pulled in $10,000 last week, you're a featured speaker for a teleseminar that's already attracted 5,000 registrants and you made your first $20,000 in 3 days, Brittany only wants to know how you are going to help her make at least $500 a week from here on out. To persuade Brittany to invest in ICU, you'll need to show her what you can do for her and back it up with how you've helped people like her get the results she wants.

Can you now see how this describing your perfect client helps you plan out the persuasive aspects of what you're writing? When you understand the challenges and problems your perfect client faces, you'll be better positioned to provide the right solutions for her. When you know which words she uses, you can adjust your language so she immediately understands what you're talking about. When you understand her objections to smacking the buy button, you'll know how to make her feel comfortable about her decision to buy. Imagining your perfect client is the foundation for persuasive writing.

Time to get all in the bid'niz

Writing to one person makes your copy more powerful – especially if you can visualize that person. About 12 years ago, one of my copywriting mentors sat me down and gave me this tip that works like a charm" tip no matter what you're selling:

"He said to picture the actual person I'm writing to. Not the audience, not the group — but the actual person. Then picture that same person stressed the HECK out. Ready to throw in the towel. Waving the white flag. And then turn your sales page into the beautiful person who comes along with the answers, sits this person down, grabs her by the hand, looks her dead in the eye and says, "Girl, I got you ... we can handle this right here and now. Let me tell you about this strategy a lot of other folks like you are using to [do whatever their heart desires]
...

In short, you should know your perfect client so well that she becomes like an imaginary bestie. You should know her so well that you can strike up a conversation with her any time. You know when she shakes her head in disagreement. You know what makes her smile and giggle. You know what questions she wants to ask. You know how to make her feel like you "get" her. That's how tight you need to be with your perfect client.

Now let's start by identifying some simple demographics for your dreamy client:

1. Is your dreamy client a woman or a man?
2. What age?
3. What profession?
4. What income is she in?
5. What education?
6. Who does she live with?
7. Does she have children?

Now let's dig deeper:

1. What social media platforms does she use?
2. What are her favorite websites?
3. What is she (or he) reading?
4. What does she dream about achieving?
5. What would she love to have?
6. What keeps her up at night?
7. What is she afraid of losing?
8. How does she make decisions?

9. What's important for her life?
10. What frustrates them most?
11. What makes her angry?
12. What's her most urgent crisis right now?
13. What humiliates them?

These questions get you thinking about your perfect client and her problems instead of your service and its features. Answer these questions and give your perfect client a name and a face. Hang your perfect client's bio close to your computer so you can see it whenever you're writing for your business; you can look at him or her and imagine you're having a deep conversation with them. Do this and your writing will become more interesting, more engaging and more persuasive.

Sounds great, Apryl. But what if I sell to other businesses? Glad you asked. Guess what? You're still selling to a person who works for that particular business. Who decides whether to invest in your services? This is your perfect client.

For example, in addition to solo service providers, I also write for mid-size technology companies and professional services firms. I don't pitch my services to "the company" because "the company" can't email me and sign my checks. Instead, I target my writing to the marketing executives responsible for deciding whether to hire me or not.

Now, if you've ever taken one of those ever-popular online business courses, you may have already gone through a ton of exercises to identify who you're writing for. But what you may not know is how to figure out who should be your perfect client – that one person who's likely to whip out her credit card and smack the buy button. In those courses or in other books, you were probably told to dig deep into your soul. Think about who lights up your soul and then write a bio, grab a picture and stick that person on the wall of your office, labeled "My Perfect Client." In theory, it sounds like a fantastic exercise. But to write copy that pierces the heart and opens the wallet of your perfect client, you have to go much further than creating her in your head.

How to find "the one"

If you address your writing to a vague audience, you'll surely water down the message and slash your sales. So finding "the one" is the most important thing you'll ever do for your business.

There's a few ways you can identify your perfect client. For instance, if you already have clients and enjoy working with a particular one, you can use him as the picture-perfect client. Simply pick up the phone (yes, even with email, people still do that) and ask her a few questions; or maybe you have a few perfect clients, and in that case, you'll pull something from each of your discussions to create a bio for your ideal client. Tell them you're doing some research into your client base. You may need to schedule a time to talk so they can give you 20 or 30 minutes to share what's important to them.

Haven't landed your first client yet? No worries, just ask a few of your email subscribers to take a quick questionnaire or jump on a call with you in exchange for a free or discounted service. Keep in mind that you learn more from open-ended questions, so limit the number of multiple-choice questions if you go the questionnaire route. Typeform and Wufoo are inexpensive, easy-to-use survey tools.

No email list? Ask a few questions in Facebook, LinkedIn or other online business forums (make sure the audience includes a reasonable number of people interested in the kinds of services you offer and not just colleagues who all do what you do). Or you can read comments in groups or blogs (if it matches your dream client), or browse through Amazon reviews. As you can see, there's a ton of ways to crawl inside your perfect client's head.

Because folks get so caught up on perfection, I always say, "perfection paralyzes your purpose" because when you focus on perfection, you prevent yourself from moving forward. Nothing we do is written in stone, so the bio you craft of your perfect client today can be refined as you mature as an entrepreneur. Commit to starting with what you know and uncovering more details later.

The more you can learn about your ideal client, the more persuasive your writing will become. You can visualize her when writing emails to your contact list, social media updates, blog posts, website copy, and even when you choose how to market your services. If your ideal client likes hanging out on Facebook rather than Pinterest, you know you don't need to spend a ton of time pinning. See how this works? When you know who you're talking to you not only make more money, but you also save time by knowing exactly how and where to spend it. And, as a solo entrepreneur, time is something you can never have too much of.

Your get-your-butt-in-gear (GYBIG) exercise:

At the end of every Copy Shot, I'll assign you an exercise to apply what I talked about to make your own writing more persuasive. No worries though, I won't be checking your homework because I believe in the "honor" system. If you do the work, you'll be honored with more clients. If you don't, well ... let's just not think about that.

GYBIG Exercise 1: Describe Your Perfect Client

Create a 1- to 2-paragraph bio describing your perfect client. Write down your answers to the questions listed earlier in this chapter. Once you have a general idea, I want you to go back and refine the bio by talking to one or two of your best clients. Ask them what made them choose you, why your service was appealing to them. Talk about their pain and whether your copy spoke to it. If you're launching a new service and they'd be perfect for it, bring it up. Ask what she'd like to see included in the service. At what price point would she smack the buy button? Pick her brain.

No clients yet? Ask about 5 to 7 folks in a social media group or online business forum where your ideal clients hang out to talk to you or complete a quick questionnaire. Offer some sort of incentive (free 10-minute coaching session or something) to show you care about these folks taking time to help you.

Start writing your dreamy client bio today. If you wait until after you talk to clients or prospects, procrastination will have set in and you'll probably never finish the exercise. To guide you through this GYBIG exercise, download a free action sheet at:
www.baab.biz/FREEActionSheets.

Copy Shot #2

I GOT 99 PROBLEMS, CAN YOU SOLVE ONE?

"Your life is your message to the world. Make it inspiring. Write something worth reading." – Beyoncé

In the first Copy Shot, we talked about the importance of identifying your ideal client and how to go about doing that. Now, it's time to consider why she or he invests in your services. The most important lesson you'll discover in this chapter is that nobody is enamored with your company and services. Folks are enamored with themselves. They want to know how you can help them to be healthier, happier, wealthier or more productive. Which problems do you solve? How do you help your clients save money and make a bucketloads of cash? These are the critical questions you need to answer if you want to persuade people to take action. In this chapter, you'll discover:

- Why you should focus on benefits and problems
- What the difference is between features and benefits
- Why folks don't invest in your services

At the end of this chapter you'll have completed your research and planning phase and you'll be ready to start writing persuasive copy.

Why you need to focus on benefits and problems

Undoubtedly your soul smiles every single time you talk about your business, your services and your work. Maybe you're excited about the new course you just launched to help folks create dazzling DIY designs. Or you just learned a new skill and packaged up all your wisdom into a badass eBook. You're selling your course or eBook, so naturally you want to flood your sales page with all the incredible features of these awesome products. Right?

Nope. The cold, hard truth is that nobody cares about you, your services or your info products. Sounds crude I know, but it's true. Folks are only interested in themselves. Here's a quick story that demonstrates the power of "selling" the benefit:

Some time ago, I dropped my SUV off at the dealership for annual service. The customer before me was dropping off a 325i (BMW) and needed a loaner. So the rep radioed for the folks in the back to pull around a 325i loaner, and this was when it got interesting.

The customer told the clerk he didn't want to drive a 325i (even though it was the same car he owned). He wanted an X5 (the SUV). And the clerk said, "Sir, we give out loaners on a first come, first serve basis and we usually only loan out the sedans." He insisted he didn't want to drive the sedan. So they're going back and forth and then the entire conversation shifted when the customer calmly said this:

"I'm considering upgrading my car and want to get the full experience of the SUV."

I still remember cracking up as the receptionist sprang into immediate action. She was on the phone, the walkie-talkie, emailing any and everybody trying to get this man an X5. See what happened here? Even though, as the customer, he was supposed to get his way, the rep wasn't going to budge until he told her something that was a benefit for BMW. She didn't care if he didn't want to drive the loaner sedan while his car was serviced. She didn't care what he dreamed about driving. But she absolutely cared when he said he was considering making another purchase with BMW.

Want folks to care about what you're selling? Give them a look inside and let them see for themselves how it will benefit them. What they'll get from it is what they want to hear, and that's what will have them begging to buy from you. To do that, you first need to make sure you're satisfying your ideal client's self-interests.

All buyers want to know how you can help them do one or several of these things:

- Save time
- Cut costs
- Rake in more cash
- Live a happier life
- Make better use of their time and resources
- Become healthier
- Lower stress
- Work less and have more leisure time

You have to ask yourself what problems your service solves and which of the results your buyer will be able to achieve after working with you. And you must be honest with yourself about the answer. Only then will you uncover how to persuade folks to buy.

Oh and don't just assume, for instance, saving money motivates your perfect client. I'll never forget I met this guy on Facebook who was offering an online marketing course. I thought a copywriter and marketing guy partnering up would be like the dynamic duo so I reached out to him. He jumped the gun and immediately went into sales mode. He went on and on about how his course was inexpensive and one of the lowest cost courses on the market. Blah, blah, blah. I stopped him and asked, "Well, what will I get out of it?" He kept on yapping about the price. I asked again, "What's the value, what results can I expect?" He replied about the price. I finally was like, "Dude, I don't care about your low price, money doesn't fascinate me. I spend it when I need to and hold on to it when it's in my best interest to do so."

This guy had no clue what his perfect client was looking for. I had the money to pay whatever price he was asking for, but first he needed to explain what I could expect to receive in return. Not just access to his course, but what results could I expect to achieve, what problems would I be able to solve, what challenges would I overcome?

Here's the thing you may not know because you're so intrigued by the services you offer: features, technical specifications and even benefits are boring. Writing only about rainbows and sunshine and "paradise" outcomes slowly lulls your perfect client to sleep because nothing grabs her by the eyeballs and commands her attention like drama. Think about it – how many "happy" shows do you watch on TV? Are you more drawn to "ratchet" reality TV shows where somebody's always fighting or sleeping with someone else's man? Are you intrigued when the newscaster talks about a controversial statement a politician made?

If so, you're just like most humans in the world – we're intrigued by drama. Now that's not to say we don't love a happy ending, but we like hearing about the drama or problems that led up to the happy ending. You see, a problem gets your ideal client's blood pressure up, gets her excited, and makes her pay attention to the "happy ending" you sell as a result of working with you. You can't just write about paradise; you also need to talk about the hassle you fight off, the headaches you cure and the glitches you prevent. The brilliant twist is that most benefits can be re-engineered as a problem you avoid.

For example, let's say you design WordPress websites which allow your client to easily make changes to her content any time she wants without the need of calling you. Or maybe you sell access to a membership site that houses a ton of business advice in one place so new entrepreneurs avoid wasting hours searching for information on Google. Or maybe you facilitate an online course that teaches entrepreneurs how to DIY their own dazzling branded images so they don't bust their shoestring budget hiring an expensive designer.

So should you play up a straightforward benefit or write more about the prevention of a problem? Even though some copywriters may tell you to "sell the pain," there's truly no right or wrong answer here. It depends on what appeals more to your ideal client. As I mentioned earlier, you can't talk only about rainbows and sunshine, but deciding to play up benefits over problems will be determined by what your ideal client is most likely to react to. If you're unsure what he or she will react to, ask your clients or test out different versions of your copy.

The difference between features and benefits

The battle between features and benefits is real. The explanation sounds simple: features are indisputable, quantifiable facts about your services. Benefits are the value your service brings to your dreamy client. However, for some reason, features and benefits are often mixed up, leaving a confused mess of copy.

Let me explain. You'll hear professional copywriters preach to their clients to "talk about the features and sell the benefits." You've probably heard this classic line: "sell the sizzle and not the steak." But what exactly does that mean? Before I answer that, let's take a minute to chat about faux benefits. Faux benefits don't truly intrigue your buyer.

For example, let's say you offer dog sitting services. One of your special features is your availability. The advantage of this special feature is that you're available 24 hours a day, 7 days a week. The benefit is that a dog owner can hire you to watch little Fi-Fi whether she's stepping out for a night with the girls or being whisked away on a romantic weekend with her man.

Now imagine you're a marketing consultant based in Cleveland, who contracts with local law firms. Because you're local, you can meet with clients easily and gain a better understanding of their business, and therefore create a marketing campaign that personifies their brand. None of these advantages are true benefits. To find the benefit, ask yourself, So what? If you do it right, that conversation will look like this:

Statement?: *You're based on Cleveland so it's easy to meet with local clients.*

So what?: *You gain a better understanding of their business.*

So what?: *You can create marketing campaigns that are better aligned with their business and culture.*

So what?: *The campaign can target the right local audience and your client can generate more revenue.*

Nothing faux about that benefit right there! Remember the list of top things all clients want from a few pages back? Generating more revenue is something clients are excited about doing. The secret to the "So What? Test" is to keep asking until you land on a real benefit.

The So What? Test can also help you shine like a superstar in verbal conversations. For instance, I was at a networking event some time ago, where I met this very bright and professional woman who introduced herself like this:

"Hi, I'm "Trisha," and I'm a freelance marketing consultant for professional services firms."

And then came that uncomfortable silence. You see, I was waiting for her to say something more, hit me with a spine-tingling sentence, give me a string of words that made me beg for her business card. But the "something more" never came.

There was no oomph or magical ending to her "story." Just that boring little sentence. And I was pretty disappointed. Why? Because when you introduce yourself like that, you always leave the other person thinking, "so what?" Now before you say that's rude, consider that folks are busy. And we're selfish. (Sorry, but it's true.) This means that people never truly start listening to you until they hear something that's going to benefit them.

So what could she have said to get me all excited? Glad you asked. She could've said something like this:

> *"Hi, I'm Trisha, and law firms and accountants make serious money off of my marketing campaigns."*

OR

> *"Hi, I'm Trisha, and not a day goes by that one of my marketing clients doesn't tell me about all the new leads they've been getting since working with me."*

I already know what you're thinking ...

"Apryl, that sounds way too 'braggadocious' for me." And maybe it is for you. But if you want to "wow" people and get them to invest in you, you need to shock them into paying attention. Now had Trisha said something like the examples above, I would have hung on her every word and been dying to find out more about her work.

I didn't care about her title – that told me nothing. However, telling me about the value she delivers and why people work with her – now that's something to talk about. Ok, let's get back to writing...

So, in many cases, you can combine a problem, benefit and feature for miraculous results. For example, imagine you're a business coach who helps new part-time small business owners build up enough clientele to quit their day jobs. You work privately with clients. You offer a structured process for creating a business strategy and action plan.

Here are two examples of a problem-benefit-feature combination:

Example 1:
Avoid being stuck in a job you hate (problem)
Grow your business so you can finally leave your day job (benefit)
Actionable, private coaching sessions (feature)

Example 2:
Avoid chasing down potential clients (problem)
Position your company to attract a constant flow of fresh, new leads (benefit)
Development of an action plan to improve your sales skills (feature)

GYBIG Exercise 2: Create a List of Reasons to Buy

List all the potential reasons your ideal buyer might want to invest in your services. Don't worry about prioritizing these reasons, just get them in writing.

Go back and read the bio you wrote for Copy Shot #1 before making your list. If you were your ideal buyer, why would you let go of your hard-earned cash? And which headache would you love to avoid?

Once you've created a list of problems and benefits, take a stab at adding the features to match. To guide you through this GYBIG exercise, download a free action sheet at
www.baab.biz/FREEActionSheets.

***

As a service provider, you are the awesomeness behind your brand. Don't forget to think about what's fantastic about you. What's the benefit of working with you? Consider how you run your business, treat your clients, and your approach to handling projects. Include your personal "features" and "benefits" on the list.

Why folks aren't busting open their wallets for you

You want to be persuasive because you want to provoke people into smacking the buy button. But it's not enough to tell your audience how fabulous you are and how much they'll benefit from working with you. You also have to anticipate their objections to your claims and overcome them one by one.

You need to reassure potential buyers. Do they hesitate because they think you're too expensive? Do they think your service is a waste of their time? Or are they concerned about quality? If you have no idea, it's time to grab the phone and call a few clients or pick the brains of a few prospects, and ask these 2 questions:

1. Before you decided to hire me, what were you doubting?
2. What were the reasons you hesitated to invest right away?

GYBIG Exercise 3: Create a List of Buyer Objections

Create a list of objections. Again, be as complete as possible. Later on you can decide whether or not you need to address every objection you wrote down. Be sure you download your free action sheet to guide you through this exercise. Pick it up at
www.baab.biz/FREEActionSheets.

And that concludes the research and planning phase of your sales page. Next up: We're rolling into smacking some keys and banging out your very own persuasive copy.

Copy Shot #3

AN INDECENT PROPOSAL

"The idea is to write it so that people hear it and it slides through the brain and straight to the heart." – Maya Angelou

You're familiar with the movie, right? Robert Redford (rich man) offers Demi Moore (poor woman) the chance to make $1 million for a night of passionate sex. She's poor and although the "indecent proposal" could possibly destroy her marriage, she and Woody Harrelson (her husband) agree their relationship is strong enough to deal with any consequences of this windfall proposal. And because of their financial situation, the millionaire's offer is too irresistible to pass up. After all, the couple believe this one night could change their fortunes from here on out. You see, their weakness is lack of money, and at the time of the proposal, they are willing to do anything to solve this pretty basic "totally normal" survival problem.

While I do believe Redford's character was a snake for using his money to get what he wanted, the film delivers a powerful message about how to create an irresistible offer. You see, his offer was only irresistible because of who he delivered it to. After all, do you think a woman making six or seven figures would have accepted his proposal? What about a woman who had a husband making that kind of money?

My guess is no because money wouldn't have been enticing enough. Now, if she was attracted to him – that's a different story. But money alone would not make her want to jump in the sack with him.

And the same goes for your "indecent" offer – make it such that you present the aspects of what you're selling in a way that's so compelling it makes it easier to say "yes" than to say "no." Your proposal should explain what a person can do with your product or service AND, don't forget, what it will do for them. Remember – sexy blue eyes aren't enough; there has to be some intelligence twinkling out of them too.

Some people think the offer is relative to pushing the buy button on a sales page or that basically you get this in exchange for X amount of dollars. But an offer is way more than that. Your offer is everything you say to make people drool over what you're selling. It talks about how your prospect will use what you're selling. It gives the big picture of what your product or service will do for the prospect. It talks about the bonuses and guarantees packaged with your product or service. It discusses any payment plans you're including. And it describes the product in action.

Now, pay attention here as this is extremely important – paint the picture of the prospect actually using your product or service and give a preview of how it will eliminate the prospect's problem. Show how the prospect's life is much better now that they've purchased the product or service.

But, before we start writing your offer, let me give you some basic ground "rules." The language of your offer should always:

1. Talk less about the actual features of your product or service and MORE about the benefits of how your prospect's life will improve after investing in what you're selling.

2. Paint the picture of what your service or product can do for your prospect.

3. Use words that help them visualize what their lives will be like after using your product or service.

Make them want it

I've said a lot about the offer and to sum it up: the offer is really the heart of copy. Contrary to what most believe, it's not your product or service. It's a solution. It's a package. It's the valuable way you present your amazing service or product to the world.

You present it in an irresistible way. Make the client start drooling over it. Yes, they want it and heck yeah they feel good after parting with their money.

Now I'm sure you want to know how to create an offer like that. Well, here I'm going to give you the exact process I use in crafting irresistible offers.

Here's where we have a quick chat on the 3 primary kinds of offers:

1. **Product offer** – something tangible such as jewelry, juice or clothing

2. **Service offer** – something you do for someone such as business coaching, website designing or copywriting.

3. **Information product offer** – information you have packaged up into a tangible product such as a coaching course, an instructional video or an eBook. While these are technically products, people sometimes have a hard time putting a value on it because at the end of the day it's nothing more than information. It's not a Louis Vuitton purse; it's not a BMW; it's not some other luxury item, but it's information products that can cost tens of thousands of dollars.

No matter the type of offer you're structuring, every piece of it – the pricing structure, the guarantee, the bonuses, the compelling way you present your product or service, showing the "paradise" side of how what you're selling can make the person's life better – all of these things unite to lower the buyer's fear, hesitancy and anxiety. Let's take a closer look.

- **Pricing structure** – offering a payment plan or delayed billing option can make your service or product more attractive to the buyer who wants and needs what you're selling but doesn't have the up-front investment to afford it.

- **Guarantee** – this shifts the risk to you and lowers the buyer's fear of buying something that might not solve their problem.

- **Bonuses** – this isn't required, but even so, I want to give you some insight on the psychology of bonuses so you can best decide whether to include them in your offer or not. Bonuses extend the power of your offer. Not really earth-shattering intel, but it's true.

- **A compelling presentation** – choosing words that spark buyer emotions makes your copy more relatable and allows the prospect to visualize herself using your product or service to solve her issue.

- **A peek inside paradise** – this lowers anxiety by putting the prospect in the mindset of using the product or service and giving her a sneak preview on how it will improve her life.

Know that people are reading your copy and thinking, "Hmm, what's it going to be like if I get this?" "What's the real value?" "What's missing?" "Is it worth it?" "Is this a joke or can this person really help me solve my problem?" "What's the catch?"

The key to crafting an irresistible offer is understanding and anticipating the questions your prospect will ask as they read through your copy. By doing so, you can make sure your copy answers these questions, which will give you a much better chance of making the sale. Here are some common questions many prospects ask no matter the type of product or service:

1. What do I have to do to get this?
2. How do I buy it?
3. What's it going to cost me?
4. How can I be sure it's going to work?
5. Am I getting my money's worth?
6. What else do I get?

Depending on your product or service, your prospects may have additional questions, but answering these will get you off to a great start. So far we've covered a lot of information about what should go in your offer. Now I'm going to give you an easy 4-part formula to follow for writing your irresistible offer:

1. Describe what makes your offer unique and valuable.
2. Give more details on what makes your offer life-changing.
3. Add bonuses to sweeten the offer.
4. Bring it all together with a "promised land" statement that gives the prospect a visualization of what their life will be like after buying your product or service.

Remember our earlier discussion about the main types of offers? Let's dig a little deeper into that conversation and examine a few example offers I wrote.

The Product Offer

The purpose of this offer is to heighten the perceived and actual value of your product. Whatever product you're selling, folks are going to immediately assume "it ain't worth their hard-earned cash." The job of your offer is to show people how much your product is going to help them; how much it's going to improve their quality of life; how it's going to help them make or save money; or how much it is going to save in resources and time.

Now if you're thinking this sounds like the list of buyer wants/desires I talked about in Copy Shot #2, you're absolutely right. Understanding which of those wants are priorities for your prospects and then using the language in your offer to satisfy those specific wants and desires is the key to getting people to take the action YOU want them to take.

Here's an excerpt from the offer I wrote for my client's cold air diffuser product which just so happened to sell out faster than funnel cakes at a carnival. Her ideal buyers suffer from severe allergies and other nasal congestion issues and frequently use essential oils and diffusers to enhance the air quality in their homes. They're familiar with the many therapeutic benefits of essential oils and diffusers, but they're hesitant to invest in a more expensive product like the one my client was selling.

As we go through this excerpt, I'll talk about the 4-step formula so you can see it in action.

Step #1: Describe what makes your offer unique and valuable.

Here I include a fact about the diffuser's authenticity by mentioning it is the "only one on the market today ..." (only use statements such as this when they're true). I also compare the diffuser to a "superhero" so the buyer can easily visualize the power this new diffuser has.

Our Cold Air Diffuser is the only one on the market today that uses the game-changing nanotechnology so you squeeze every ounce of therapeutic benefit you can from your essential oils.

It's like having a superhero living in your home, one who has the power to protect you from all the junk in the world. Ooh sounds amazing, right?

Step #2: Give more details on what makes your offer life-changing.

I now move into talking about the features in a way that also positions them as benefits for the buyer – the diffuser can fit anywhere in their home, it has a remote and automatic features that make it convenient and easy to use, and it has technology that taps into every ounce of therapeutic benefit offered by the essential oils (which are put inside the diffuser).

Now you probably already know essential oils are amazing, but you may not know all the fantastic features you get with this diffuser. I'm talking:

- *A portable, sleek, compact, stylish and whisper-quiet component that's perfect for your home, office, yoga studio, and more.*
- *A remote control and built-in timers that puts the option to control the scent intensity levels at your fingertips.*
- *Automatic/programmable shut-off capability that allows you to choose from 1-, 4- and 8-hour intervals per day.*
- *Revolutionary nanotechnology that gives you access to the full therapeutic benefit of your essential oils*

Step #3: Add bonuses to sweeten the offer.

This section is loaded with even more benefits to using the product, such as peace of mind about the quality of the product, a recovery of investment, a 1-year warranty, and an exclusive 10% discount my client decided to offer for new buyers. These benefits were all positioned as bonus features the buyer would not find with other diffusers. In this section, we also included a call to action and asked for the sale.

And that's only the beginning. You also get:

- *The best therapeutic benefits ... GUARANTEED. That is because of all the goodness you get from our diffuser's mind-blowing use of nanotechnology.*
- *Over 2,000 hours per year of diffuser enjoyment, without the worry of clogging or other repair issues.*
- *Whisper-quiet and without all the "drive-me-nuts" swirling disco lights you get with other diffusers. Instead, you get a peaceful unit that works its magic for up to 8 continuous hours, so you can use it overnight for the*

best sleep ever. While other diffusers are noisy and get you ready to "bust a move" and party in the swirl of disco lights, ours will help you rest easy.

- *A recovery of your investment in as little as 2 short months—most other diffusers have stopped working by that time. And when you compare the cost of the "cheaper diffuser," which requires much more oil and will most likely stop working within a couple of months, you're saving $1440/year simply by making the right choice for your health.*

- *A sturdy diffuser made from aluminum that's designed to last 10 years and maybe longer depending on how often you use it. Our diffuser parts are made in Japan and Taiwan and only assembled in China. This is completely different from 99% of all other diffusers that are entirely manufactured in China. (See pic below)*

As if that's not enough to send you racing for your credit card, the nebulizing diffuser also comes with a 1-year warranty, paid repair services and lifetime maintenance (perks you won't find with any of the so-called diffusers from Walmart or similar stores).

Advanced technological components with this many features can easily sell for $400.00 or more. But you won't pay anywhere near that ... because I want you to live a happy, healthier life without emptying your pockets.

Click here to find out more and to claim your exclusive discount.

Step #4: Bring it all together with a "promised land" statement that gives the prospect a visualization of what their life will be like after buying your product or service.

Here, we reiterate the discount because remember, this buyer is concerned about getting the most benefits for the price. Then, we give the "promised land" statement: "... can be your ticket to a happier, healthier and more productive life." This statement summarizes what will happen when the buyer invests in my client's diffuser.

Remember, the ideal buyer is suffering from severe allergies and other health issues that are preventing him or her from fully enjoying life. This section tells the buyer that once he purchases, he will have his ticket to a better life.

Now, because I really want you to change your life, as a bonus, you'll get an exclusive discount of 10% off the current price when you buy today. Yes, our diffuser can truly be your ticket to a happier, healthier and more productive life!

The Service Offer

A ton of folks sell services. One of the biggest complaints about selling services is that other people in the market lowball their own services, which drives down the overall perceived value of it. For instance, I sell copywriting services and charge thousands of dollars for my services – because what I do is worth every penny. Now some other copywriter might think they're competing with someone who writes 1,000-word articles for $5. This is only a problem when the seller makes it a problem.

Now, my professional opinion as to why people are not able to ask for and get the money that is equal to what they're delivering is more about not being able to describe what they do in a way that conveys the true value. It's not about copywriter Angie Smith who wants to write articles for $5, it's about how the audience perceives the value of what you do. And that perception is formed by what you say in your offer.

Before writing the above example I gave for the product offer, I spent over an hour with the client talking about her ideal client, all so I understood their pain, emotions and desires. Now for the service offer example below, let's take a look at an online course one of my clients is selling.

The ideal buyer for this course is an entrepreneur or author who is a genius at what she does, but she is stuck being the best-kept secret in her industry. She wants TV exposure to promote her services, products or book but has no idea where to start. She believes a publicist could help, but she doesn't have tens of thousands of dollars to spend on a publicist just yet, so she wants to DIY her exposure. She's smart enough to she know that with some guidance she could rock the market with her mind-blowing brilliance.

So, now you know WHO we're talking to, let's take this offer through the 4-step formula. Oh, one thing before we dig in: you should know that this client is a vibrant, giddy lover-of-life who always wears a smile. As we're going through each part of the formula, I want you to notice the voice used in the writing. We'll talk more about this later, but for now, watch how I use a combination of informal and "slang" language to infuse the copy with my client's personality.

Step #1: Describe what makes your offer unique and valuable.

Here, I highlight how this program gives the buyer access to all the wisdom inside one of Hollywood's top TV producers, which means she has the credentials to guide buyers through her "do-it-with-you" program.

> *[TV Coaching] is the premier, "do-it-with-you," online coaching program where I walk you step-by-step through a proven, guaranteed process of getting you booked and on TV so that you move from being your industry's best-kept secret to well-known genius.*

> *Inside, you get the process, the pitch script for TV producers, the lingo (ever hear of a "chyron"?), the insider Hollywood secrets, the virtual hand-holding … everything!*

> *And the best part?*

> *The entire 8-week program is backed by my relationships with some of Hollywood's top TV producers, my success with coaching other "best-kept secrets" on how to get the exposure they needed to become credible, recognizable experts and my personal journey of booking myself (*repeat booking myself*) on top networks such as ABC, CBS, CW, FOX and NBC to promote my book, So You Want To Be On A Reality Show?: Insider Tips to Make the Cut..*

Step #2: Give more details on what makes your offer life-changing.

Here, I play up the buyer's pain and show why this program is perfect for her – if she's truly ready to share her genius with the world.

> *This program is right for you if:*

> *You know people will benefit from your brilliance, but you have no idea how to let them know you exist.*

You're fed up with wasting your courage on contacting TV stations and never getting a response.

You're ready to step outside your tiny corner of the world and share your genius with tens of millions of viewers.

Because repeat after me: being a best-kept secret is NOT a good secret to keep!

Step #3: Add bonuses to sweeten the offer.

On my client's sales page, this section of the offer does not immediately follow the text above in Step #2. But I wanted to show that she did include bonuses with the offer.

The purpose of these particular bonuses is to extend the value of the offer by giving buyers the knowledge to not only get TV exposure for their brands, but also to get tips to fill their pipelines.
+ 4 Absolutely Awesome Bonuses (Valued at $3500!)

- *List building guidance from the phenomenal [excluded for client privacy]*
- *Little-known revenue-generating secrets from revenue rockstar [excluded for client privacy]*
- *7 secrets to gaining side-business success from the illustrious [excluded for client privacy]*
- *How to make your brand bankable with trailblazer [excluded for client privacy]*

OMGeeee, I'm giddy just talking about this yumminess! I created this online coaching program to give you the same exact insider secrets I learned from 20 years of editing hit TV shows and from collaborating with some of Hollywood's most popular TV producers and network executives.

And every lesson is delivered in juicy, bite-size pieces.

Step #4: Bring it all together with a "promised land" statement that gives the prospect a visualization of what their life will be like after buying your product or service.

Here, I dig into the fear, hesitancy and anxiety of the buyer, reminding them of what they want and how this program will help them get it.

I play up the fact that celebrities get TV exposure easily, but this course is for everybody else. Lastly, I include a call to action and ask for the sale.

It's Your Duty to Serve Your Audience

By keeping your talents tucked away in your tiny corner of the world, you're not doing your part to serve and inspire the world. And I get it: You know you have what it takes to master your story and rock your TV segment, you just don't know how to go about doing it.

That's why if this is your dream, enrolling in this program is critical. I'll eliminate your confusion and provide you with the exact tried and tested steps to get you booked and on TV. No fluff. No BS. Just results.

But here's the key thing:

You have to show up and do the work to see results. If you're looking for a magic formula for getting booked on TV as an industry expert where you do absolutely nothing (or keep doing what you've always done), this program is not for you.

All non-celebrities not raking in enough dough to shell out tens of thousands of dollars for a pricey publicist but ready to go from best-kept secret to well-known expert, click the link below.

The key to creating an irresistible offer for a service is to think first about what the service is and what it does at the bare bones level. Then, look for unique aspects that distinguish your service from everything else the prospect could possibly consider instead. Lastly, think about the most innovative and least expensive things you can add to your core service in order to pump up the perceived value.

Now, the smartest entrepreneurs will figure out the offer first, before they write their headline, before they bang out the bullets, before they do anything else. Then they write persuasive copy around the offer. It's truly the easiest and fastest way to craft a great sales page. Just to recap, the offer is a combination of features and benefits that show the product or service in action – in a compelling way that captivates the heart, mind and pockets of the RIGHT prospect, someone who is qualified and ready for the solution you're offering.

GYBIG Exercise 4: Craft Your Irresistible Offer

Craft your very own irresistible offer. In this Copy Shot, you received a ton of detail about what an offer is, what it should include and how critical it is to deliver your offer in a compelling way. Now, let me do a quick recap on the main 4 steps to writing an irresistible offer:

1. Describe what makes your offer unique and valuable.
2. Give more details on what makes your offer life-changing.
3. Add bonuses to sweeten the offer.
4. Bring it all together with a "promised land" statement that gives the prospect a visualization of what their life will be like after buying your product or service.

For today's exercise, use the 4-step formula above to craft a new offer or to boost the perceived value of an existing offer. Remember to think about the most unique and valuable qualities of your offer and describe those things at the most basic level.

To guide you through this GYBIG exercise, download a free action sheet at www.baab.biz/FREEActionSheets.

***

The Ultimate Secret to Persuasive Writing

Your first GYBIG exercise was to simply put your raw offer in writing. Don't worry about how it sounds. Don't worry about using the "perfect" words – just write it down. Now, here I'm going to give you the ultimate secret to help you make it so compelling that it gets your prospect racing to smack the buy button.

So, by now, you should have noticed something very distinct about this book. You may have heard copywriting principles here and there, yet this persuasive writing book delivers something different from the others.

What am I talking about?

I'm talking about FLAVA, PERSONALITY, SWAG, ladies and gentlemen. I am talking PIZAZZ!

As you read these words here, you probably get a feel for my personality. The "flava" secret is one of the most essential ingredients to persuasive writing. People buy from folks they like. When you infuse your writing with personality, people feel like they know you. This sense of intimacy leads to trust. And when they like you, rapport comes along and before you know it – you make the sale.

Every great writer I know writes in their own voice. Maya Angelou writes like Maya Angelou. Stephen King writes like Stephen King. Famous copywriter Dan Kennedy writes like Dan Kennedy. Speaking of copywriters, our magic is not only writing in our own voices, but studying the voices and services of our clients so we perfect their voice as well. Now, I don't want you to be concerned about writing in any voice other than your own. Just remember, if you're in the market to hire a copywriter and you meet anyone who tells you they can't write in a way that sounds like you – RUN! FAST!

Wanna know the best way to lace your writing with your own special swag? WRITE LIKE YOU TALK. Don't attempt to be the best communicator or a prolific writer – simply be you. It's truly the fastest way to master persuasive writing without the need for special tricks, templates or blueprints.

Why? Well, because you already know how to talk. Let's say you and I were having a conversation over a drink, just talk like that. You can use slang, swear words and your normal lingo. Don't try to be overly professional. Add some flava and be a little "incorrect."

You know what? This is one of the most powerful lessons I've learned in copywriting. It's not only a proven way to boost sales, but it brings you a ton of freedom to be your authentic self. You're no longer fishing around the Internet for the "perfect" words that sell; NO! you're simply having a normal everyday conversation in writing.

The other great thing about writing like you talk is it sets you apart from the hundreds of thousands of other "competitors" in your industry. No one can steal your swag when you're selling in a super crowded place like the Internet. Remember, it's all you because no one has you, only you have full dibs on that one.

GYBIG Exercise 5: Examine Your Offer Lingo

Go back and look at your offer you just wrote in Exercise 1 and pay attention to the language you used. Are you being too techie? Are you using language your audience will easily understand? Are you being too formal and uptight? The language you use should feel like a real conversation with your prospect. To help with this exercise, you may want to tap a client or two to check out your offer before releasing it into the world. They can read through your copy and let you know if it's clear, straightforward and engaging.

To guide you through this GYBIG exercise, download a free action sheet at www.baab.biz/FREEActionSheets.

Copy Shot #4

THE B.O.S.S. SALES PAGE MAP

"Your life is your message to the world.
Make it inspiring. Write something worth reading." –
Beyoncé

Early on in my copywriting career, I was fortunate enough to have some really great mentors and access to stacks of fantastic books on the craft of persuasive writing. The problem was that most of them started out much like this book. Tons of useful tips but no boilerplate templates that I could just "fill-in-the-blank" to bang out a profitable sales page.

As such, I don't want you to end this book feeling like "damn, I still need a guide, a template, a map ... something." That's why in this Copy Shot, I decided to take you on a guided tour through the wonderful world of crafting powerful, smack-the-buy-button sales pages each and every time.

Let's get to it. Note that along the way, we'll make 5 stops through "sales page" land, and as a result you'll end the tour with an easy-to-follow map for whenever you want to relive our beautiful journey together. Now, in order for you to be successful with this roadmap, I highly recommend you build on the steps I outlined earlier in this book:

1. **Copy Shot #1** – crafting your "ideal client" bio
2. **Copy Shot #2** – drilling down into the benefits of your product or service
3. **Copy Shot #3** – creating your irresistible offer and writing like you talk

Remember, I said writing your sales page around your offer is the fastest and easiest way to write your copy. Now that you have this sales page roadmap, you can bet you'll have a much easier time outlining your page and revising it to "perfection."

Over time, you'll notice that your brain will automatically think about this map whenever you write copy. And this is when you'll really be able to churn out fast and compelling copy.

So that you fully grasp how this map works, I'll be providing explanations throughout each section along with recommendations for words/phrases that are virtually guaranteed to boost the likelihood of making the sale.

If you have any questions about this or any of the topics covered in this book, feel free to contact me at <u>abeverly@baab.biz</u>.

Sound cool?

Alrighty then, let's get to it!

The B.O.S.S. Sales Page Roadmap

Now that you've finished your irresistible offer, it's time to write the rest of your sales page around it. Here are the core parts I include in every sales page I write for clients:

1. Headline
2. Lead
3. Offer
4. Backstory
5. Close

Nothing world-class about it, is there? Yet, my guess is you'll find that my simple map for creating sales pages makes banging out one profitable page after another way easier, and maybe even "routine" – routine is a good thing here.

Oh, by the way, B.O.S.S. is an acronym that forms the foundation of everything I write. It's about being BOLD, OUTSPOKEN, SINCERE and the SUPERSTAR you were born to be. Timid folks don't win in business ... but BOSSES do. That's why I push my clients to write like a B.O.S.S.

OK then, let's start with headlines. The first step to writing headlines is ... forgetting the idea of crafting headlines that "hook." In fact, avoid writing headlines your peers consider "catchy" or "killer." Your only objective is to write a headline that gets your sales page READ, not to get your peers raving in Facebook groups about how you "hit the mark." And to get your sales page read, you must know your ideal client's struggles and then reveal the solution. There truly is no more "killer" headline than that. Now, you could use die-hard tricks and fancy language, but tapping into your ideal client's problems and addressing them will get your page READ every time.

So to that end, pull out your client bio from the exercise in Copy Shot #1. This bio is golden because it lays out your prospect's problems, desires and wants. Go ahead and whip that baby out and let's get to writing your headline.

The Headline

Before we dig into a few sample headlines, please allow me to bust a few myths:

- **Myth #1 – the job of the headline is to SELL.** This couldn't be further from the truth. The sole purpose of the headline is to get folks to read the first line of body copy. Anything beyond that, and you got your headline working overtime.

- **Myth #2 – "killer" headlines SELL.** The only thing "killer" headlines can do is kill your sales. You see, what you peers, colleagues and even other copywriters may see as a smart headline probably doesn't appeal to your ideal clients. You don't want folks praising you for the quality of the headline. You want folks READING the page.

- **Myth #3 – body copy is more important than the headline.** Hmm, if you want people to actually READ your sales page (and I'm betting you do), you better have a darn good headline.

Now that we know what to say in your headline, it's time to move on to how to phrase it so the prospect starts reading the sales page.

Every copywriter you meet will have a list of tried and tested headlines they've stored as the best examples of headlines ever written. The thing about this is because each headline is carefully crafted with a specific buyer in mind, using "tried and tested" headlines probably won't work for your page. But when you use the "issue-solution" method, you pretty much will always write a great headline. Why? Because the issue-solution headline method is customized to identify the issue YOUR buyer is facing and presents a SOLUTION to that specific problem. You can never, ever go wrong when you're showing folks that you understand their struggle and have a solution to fix it.

Let's look at this in action …

Headline Sample #1:

The Pain-Free Playbook for Winning Clients on Social Media
Go from Social Media Overwhelm to Social Media "Oh Yeah!" in as
Little as 3 Hours

Can you easily identify what the ideal buyer for this playbook is struggling with? If you said "social media overwhelm" – you're absolutely right! How about the solution?

Ding, ding, ding! You said the "Pain-Free Playbook" and yay, you win again!

All jokes aside, this headline is certainly going to get the attention of a buyer who has been spending a ton of time on social media with no results – they're not attracting clients, making money, raising awareness … none of that.

Headline Sample #2:

**Think You Need to Hire a Publicist or Be a Celebrity to Get
Booked on TV and Share Your Genius with Millions?**

This is a longer headline without the subheading. Again, can you easily guess the issue? How about the solution?

Really you are so smart I know you just blurted this out:

Issue: Stuck feeling like the only way to get on TV is to have a publicist or be a celebrity.

Solution: Wants to build brand awareness by getting booked on TV.

Ya'll are on fiyah! OK, just one more …

Headline Sample #3:

Busy Mom's Guide to Baby Sleep Training
The nighttime, crying, screaming, hungry, teething, baby-can't-fall-
asleep-without-mama, so you can rest course.

Some entrepreneurs love using the title of their courses or products as the headline for the sales page. This sample shows that framework in action. The client wanted to keep her course title as the headline so I added a subheading that got mamas excited about reading the sales page.

Alright, same as before. What's the issue and solution here?

Issue: Working moms are exhausted from being up all night with fussy babies.

Solution: This course addresses nearly every possible reason the baby could be fussy in the middle of the night – crying, screaming, hungry, teething, baby-can't-fall-asleep-without-mama – and tells the buyer she can finally rest after getting what's inside this course.

Bonus Tip: Sometimes writing a quick headline first helps you to lay it out and decide what the page is going to look like. Then once you have completed what you want on the page you can always go back and adjust your headline.

The Offer

The offer includes your pricing structure, the guarantee, bonuses, the compelling way you present your product or service, and the "paradise" side of how what you're selling can make the buyer's life better. Now, aren't you doing the happy dance right now because you wrote your offer back in Copy Shot #3? Yay!

Now, one thing I want to talk about here is how to lead into the offer so it flows with the rest of your sales page. I have 3 easy-peasy options:

Offer Lead-in Option #1:

That's exactly why I created/launched/developed [insert name of product or service] ...

Offer Lead-in Option #2:

Introducing ...

Offer Lead-in Option #3:

But here's the good news ...

I swear you really can't get any easier than these. And with that, we are moving right along ...

The Lead

You can start your sales page with either a reiteration of the pain the buyer is experiencing or through an "I" story. Now, there's a rumor floating around out there in copywriting land that it's never okay to use "I" stories in persuasive writing. Ever see a story that got passed around the room and got all mixed up by the time it reached the last person? This is one of those times.

While you certainly want to focus on the buyer, "I" stories help you, as the "expert," to establish a connection by conveying empathy. The fact is, folks are afraid of salespeople. They think they're always up to something to weasel them out of their cash. But then again, they like relatable people who are personable, considerate and helpful. Telling "I" stories helps you become that person in writing.

Let's take a look at a few lead examples:

Lead Sample #1:

Times It's Okay to Ignore Your Kids

Sounds crazy, right?

I mean what "real" mom would ever ignore her kids?

Wait, now before you give me the side eye, I've got a quick story for you that sounds like something right out of a Lifetime movie about a "not-so-good mother."

You see, I thought I could "reschedule" time with my son to accommodate my growing list of clients and speaking engagements. I was in straight "beast mode" — transforming the lives of businesswomen and booking high-profile presentations — all the while my son just wanted us to get some sand between our toes and have fun.

But the entrepreneur side of me was on a mission. And vacation could wait … or so I thought. Now, here's where everything went wrong.

My ex decided he didn't want to bob and weave with my schedule. And based on our custody agreement, he had that right. So that left me scrambling to find a "good" time to hang out with my own son.

Anyway, long story short, after that little situation …

I was sure I'd earned the "Bad Mom of the Year" Award.

That my son wasn't going to love me anymore, and my family would whisper around me, "Ooh, girl, did you hear what Jenenne did … "

Now, I've been fired from a job. Stuck in the grocery store line with the clerk saying, "Ma'am, your card's been declined." But none of that compares to how horrifying it was to let my son down.

Believe me, it was one of the most nightmarish experiences I've ever had as a mom.

But you know what?
It got me to thinking about you.

What would YOU do if your business partner called about a last-minute priority project and you already agreed to play Monopoly with your kids?

I left the headline is this lead sample since the lead plays off the headline. See how the coach talks about herself but the story is so compelling you can't seem to stop reading? You're dying to find out what she did to her kid and when you least expect it – BOOM – that last line starts leading into the offer.

Lead Sample #2:

You've heard all the horror stories about the "zombie babies" who never. Ever. Sleep!

Heck, you may have even secretly blamed a mama for not being able to cure her little one's sleep problems.

But now ...

You're the exhausted mama whose sweet baby is waking up 7 times a night (or more)!

You've already talked to the pediatrician, read a stack of highly recommended baby sleep books, and watched several "baby whisperer" videos that tell you exactly what you can do.

Trouble Is,
You Don't Know How To Do Any of It.

So you're worn out (and frustrated). Maybe you've spent countless nights nursing, cuddling and rocking. Or you tried the swaddle method, but like Houdini, she wiggled out and started screaming just as you drifted off to sleep. Or perhaps you read it's best to let him "cry it out" and that was simply another sleepless (and catastrophic) night.

But What If I Told You My Baby Sleep Method Is Guaranteed
To Get Your Lil' Night Owl To Sleep 5 or More (Straight) Hours
So You Can Rest?

In this lead sample, I start out by painting the picture of the buyer's painful existing situation. The prospect is moving down the page, nodding to each painful memory of the night before and just before she sinks into a deep depression, here comes the solution. Now, you have to be careful not to drown the prospect in her sorrows by dragging out the painful story. Make sure you give just enough to say, "I understand," and then reveal the solution.

Lead Sample #3:

Are you ready to finally turn your incredible story into a smash-hit reality TV show (and make some of that show creator money)?

Before you answer, first imagine how having tens of millions of viewers around the world tuning in every single week to watch YOUR show would feel.

OMGeeeee! I got goosebumps just thinking about it and am sure you did too.

Now, I want you to think about where you are today. Does any of this sound familiar?

You know your show idea is "beast," but you don't know anything about developing it into an irresistible storyline with addictive characters.

You heard someone mention the importance of choosing a show "genre" and you're clueless ... and way too embarrassed to even ask what the heck a "genre" is.

You're tired of just "talking about it" and are about 10 seconds away from calling up the networks and saying, "Hey, my show idea rocks!" But then WHAT?

Here's the honest truth, you're stuck.

And that means ...

Your idea will continue to sit in your back pocket while you tune in every week to watch somebody else's reality show.

Sounds like a pretty sad story, right? But since I'm all about taking action, how about we get back to answering:

"Are you ready to finally turn your incredible story into a smash-hit reality TV show (and make some of that show creator money)?"

If you said, "Heck yeah!" then keep reading because you're about to find out exactly how to go from "beast" idea to smash-hit show!

Now, in this lead, we start out with a glimpse inside the "promised land." You can do this easily by saying "Imagine/picture this ..." and then you go straight into what life would be like AFTER the prospect buys your product or service.

Each of these leads has its own nuances and there's no right or wrong one to use. But again, you must go with the flow that will be most appealing to your ideal client. I know I sound like a song in your playlist on repeat, but it's true. None of this stuff will work unless it is tailored to what your prospects want (and don't want).

The Backstory

This section is where you tell the prospect who you are and why they should believe and trust you. The key is to present your backstory in a way that's helpful and not boastful.

Here are a few samples:

Backstory Sample #1:

In case we haven't had the pleasure of meeting yet ...

Greetings. I'm Ms. Wonderful Coach — mom, transformational speaker, coach, author and CEO of Wonderful Coaching. I guide entrepreneurs, heart-centered women and celebrities through a spiritual yet practical journey on how to embrace their value, transform their perspective on self-worth, stand in their power, unlock their passion, and create a fulfilling life of wealth and happiness.

My clients have generated well over $2 million in revenue. And you know what they all have in common ...

They all took action. They didn't wait around for something big to happen to them. They didn't use being a mom as an excuse.

They believed in themselves. Listened to their intuition. And made big things happen.

If you're genuinely committed to having it all — I invite you to do the same.

Take. Action. Now.

See how the backstory talks about the coach's credentials without bragging? See how I wrote it in a way that flips the focus back to the buyer? This is what you want to do. Don't go on and on about yourself, but do make sure you're engaging the prospect by flipping it back to her.

Backstory Sample #2:

Hi, I'm Suzie Smith, business strategist, speaker & author. Also, entrepreneur, dog lover and a massive fun-seeker.

After spending 20 years in a very successful corporate career, I joined the entrepreneurial ranks. I've built several businesses and I'm in love with my current 6-figure business.

I'm passionate about helping women entrepreneurs better structure, leverage and run their businesses. And I loooooo-ve to live brave & bold, stepping into spaces that scare the sh&$ out of me. For me, life is all about having FUN, living life MY way and teaching other boss ladies how to do the same.

See how this backstory oozes with the consultant's personality? Instead of coming off as pushy and sleazy, she's conversing like your "homegirl" who just so happens to be a GENIUS in all things business strategy. Sounds like a great friend to have, right?

Is your brain bursting with ideas on how you can effectively communicate your own backstory? Hold on, grasshopper – we got one more sample ...

Backstory Sample #3:

I'm Jane Doe, and like you I listened to all the lies my doctor told me about what would relieve my seasonal allergy symptoms. I mean, he prescribed every allergy medicine imaginable—but nothing worked. And then, all that changed when I ditched my pill-pushing doctor and opted for natural remedies.

You see, I moved to the United States in 2007. Nearly half a year after the big move, I got bit by the nasty "allergy bug" and I was devastated. I was sick nearly every other week – runny nose and itchy eyes, nose, ears and throat, as well as wheezing, restlessness and fatigue. Argh!!

So I did what most people do: I went to see an allergist. And as you probably imagined, I tested positive for a variety of allergens. Funny thing is, I never, ever suffered from allergies until I moved to the United States, where 55% of the population tests positive for one or more allergens.

My doc prescribed allergy shots and pills. For 5 long years, I popped pills and sucked up my disdain for getting stuck in the arm with long, pointy needles. And after spending thousands of dollars on worthless treatments and losing tens of thousands of dollars in lack of productivity, I said enough is enough.

I opened up to the therapeutic benefits of natural remedies after attending a health seminar hosted by the amazing Tony Robbins. I paid thousands to hear about the many benefits of essential oils and would happily do it again because I've been allergy-free for 3 years now.

Here's what happened:

I found out the reason for my allergies was NOT the environment and weather (like the doc said). It was the chemicals in my food, toiletries and household cleaning products. And when I did the "crazy" thing of switching to organic foods and products, natural supplements and essential oils, guess what happened?

My allergy symptoms vanished!

You see, once I stopped believing the lies my doc told me, I began to cure what was ailing me. And now, I feel better than ever. All because I stopped poisoning my body with artificial treatments and harmful chemicals found in the foods most of us eat every single day.

That, my friend, is why I started this program:

To bust all the doctor myths and tell you the truth —
when you stop consuming "garbage,"
you can live a better, healthier life just like I do.

This client had a very detailed backstory but it works because she's connecting prospects who are experiencing the same issues. And then right as the story wraps up, she tells them she just wants to help others find the same relief as her only much faster and with far less pain.

The Closer

In the closer, you simply want to requalify why investing in your product or service is the BEST move for your prospect. And ask for, the sale. Even though you will have buy buttons strategically placed through the sales page, you want to officially ask for the sale in the closing.

Again, we're not going for pushy, sleazy. We're going for personable helpful and empathetic. Here are a few highly effective options for closing the sale in writing:

Closer Sample #1:

> *But here's the key thing:*
>
> *You have to show up and do the work to see results. If you're looking for a magic formula for making it big in reality TV where you do absolutely nothing (or keep doing what you've always done), this masterclass is not for you.*
>
> *All non-celebrities with a "beast" show idea ready to break into the world of reality TV, click the link below.*

I call this closer the "qualifier." This is probably one of the least used closers. But it's pretty effective when done right. Why? I'm not sure. But for some reason folks like to be told why they don't "qualify" for something. It gets them pumped up to show you they're not the "lazy" people you're talking about.

Closer Sample #2:

Your 7-Day "Sleep Like A Baby" Money Back Guarantee

> *I'm so confident you'll learn the exact steps to get your baby sleeping through the night, I'm offering a 7-day money back guarantee. Buy the course today and if you're not completely happy with it, turn in your completed homework within 7 days of your purchase date for a full refund. No questions asked. This way, you got nothing to lose (except for those wretched 3 a.m. feedings)!*

Now, contrary to popular "expert" opinion, you don't always need a guarantee. I, for one, don't always include guarantees, but you'll have to test it out and see what works best with your peeps.

Closer Sample #3:

This Package ROCKS

Get 14 glorious hours of exclusive interviews with 13 of the world's most successful coaches – all in an easy-to-download MP3 format.

Get it for just $XX

Or for my action-taking entrepreneurs:

This Package is SUPER AWESOME

Get 14 glorious hours of exclusive interviews with 13 of the world's most successful mompreneurs – all in an easy-to-download MP3 format.

PLUS
13 downloadable transcripts of all 14 hours of recordings.

Access to the Exclusive After-Party where you'll get the never-before-heard scoop from all the successful coaches I interviewed. (You won't be able to get these kinds of insider secrets anywhere else.)

And a chance to win a $500.00 Amazon gift card (winner will be announced at the exclusive after-party).

Come on in now!

Remember, the price jumps to $XX after February 29.

Here I highlight the "awesomeness recap." Now this is obviously not a real offer recap, but you get the point, right? This kind of closer is a great way to remind prospects one last time about all the juicy stuff they're getting. You can also put the details in a spiffy graphic to streamline the page.

There's a ton of ways to close your sales page – pick one that feels right for you and your prospects.

And that's it for the B.O.S.S. Sales Page Map, buddy.

GYBIG Exercise 6: Write Your Sales Page Like a B.O.S.S.

Go back through each of the parts of a sales page and write each section. Don't race to get this done – focus on one or two components a day over the next week.

To guide you through this GYBIG exercise, download a free B.O.S.S. Sales Page Checklist at www.baab.biz/FREEActionSheets.

This Copy Shot should get you off to a running start crafting a profitable sales page. However, there is still much more you can learn to crank up your response. In the meantime, for more advanced copywriting info check out www.baab.biz/copymakeover-2.

Copy Shot #5

YOU AIN'T DONE... YET

"You don't always have to know exactly what you're doing, or where you're going. You just have to be willing to take the next step. Sometimes clear and powerful, sometimes with blind unwavering faith." – Lisa Nichols

Have you finished a draft of your sales page? Fantastic. But you ain't done yet because now it's time to start editing. You see, editing is like completing your outfit with a fresh new pair of heels or accessorizing it with a beautiful designer handbag. Sure the outfit might look alright without the new stilettos and purse, but when you refine your look with those additions, you make yourself irresistible.

Same goes for your copy. It might be alright as a draft, but when you take the time to edit what you wrote, you're more likely to make your copy more appealing, more persuasive and more mesmerizing. And being more of those things means you increase your chances of making the sale.

In this chapter, you'll discover:

- Why nobody's reading your web copy
- 4 ways to make your content more engaging and compelling
- The 5 most common copywriting mistakes of all time
- How to edit your copy so it sings the tune your peeps want to hear

At the end of this chapter, you'll get a checklist to edit your sales page so you can be super sure you don't miss a thing.

Nobody "reads" online

Picture a middle-aged woman who just spotted a gray strand while brushing her hair. She moves up close to the mirror to see if there are any more gray "cousins" hanging out. She notices everything not quite right. She has a gray hair in her right eyebrow. She found two more strands of gray hair on the left side of her head. And oh no, there's six more right where she normally parts her hair!

When writing and editing copy for the web, you're analyzing everything about it – just like the woman inspecting her hair in the mirror. But keep in mind, that's not how browsers treat your copy.

Text shared on the web is scanned or glanced at – certainly not read word-for-word. Browsers are on the hunt for information, services or products, and they make split decisions based on what they find.

Usability expert Jakob Nielsen suggests that on the average web page, users have time to read at most 28% of the words; 20% is more likely. So while you're slaving over each and every word on your sales page, prospects are scanning the page to see if your product or service can address the problem they want to solve.

Well, Apryl, if that's the case, why do I even bother with editing?

What a great question, thanks for asking.

To get your message across and let the right prospect know she's in the right place, you need simple statements that require as little thinking as possible. Being too clever can require your prospects to think too hard about what you're trying to say.

You want to write for a 12-year-old (minus the emojis and text abbreviations ☺) so your text is easy to follow. Now, everyone always asks me about putting slang and curse words in their copy. My answer is if you use the words in everyday conversations **<u>AND</u>** you're absolutely certain your audience understands the slang you're using and is not offended by curse words – go for it.

You can't possibly please everyone, nor should you try. But the last thing you want to do is piss off an ideal client because you put "f*$k" in your copy, not because you love the word but because you saw a competitor using the word and thought you'd try it too. Bad move – remember when I said the ultimate secret to persuasive writing is adding your own personality … not someone else's.

Here are a few more tips to make your copy compelling and easy on the eyes:

1. "Chunkify" your copy – six lines max for each paragraph.
2. Keep sentences short – aim for 14 words on average. (Fun fact: the American Press Institute found that readers can understand more than 90% of the information in sentences with 9-14 words. Comprehension dropped to 10% in 43-word sentences.)
3. Avoid repeating the exact same text on different pages – it's annoying.
4. Clear the clutter – try to cut at least 20 to 40% of your text

during the editing phase.

Hit List for Top 5 Copywriting Mistakes of All Time

Did you see comedian Chris Rock's 2014 movie Top Five? In the movie, Chris Rock and his friends get together and argue over the top 5 greatest rappers of all time. Back when it was released, this movie sparked a movement of DJs everywhere trying to get celebrities and radio show guests to give up their Top 5 picks.

Even though most folks will never, ever agree on a Top 5 list of rappers, most copywriters will agree on this list of Top 5 copywriting mistakes. And here they are listed below, in no particular order, because as far as great copywriters are concerned, they are all equally terrible.

Mistake #1: Committing poetic injustice

Rhythmic, poetic prose is beautiful in a pop or rap song – but not so lovely in business content. You have no need to camouflage your service or product behind clever writing. Give it to the prospect straight so she can make the right choice and get on with using your service or product.

Mistake #2: Loving you (too much)

I was watching Bill Maher's hilarious HBO talk show Real Time the other night, and he said something to his ride-or-die audience members that pierced my heart:

"I'm not here for me, I'm here for you."

And that's exactly how you should feel whenever you write copy for your business. It's not about what you want and what you want to put on the page. It's about what your ideal clients want and what they want to see on the page.

Mistake #3: Being too shy for the sale

Ever hear folks say you're "too cool for school?" School isn't a fashion show – you get your butt in a seat, open your ears and learn. Same goes for selling. Making the sale isn't about being timid or shy. If you want the sale, you must ask for it. No matter how much your prospect needs what you're selling, most of them aren't going to beg you to take their money.

Mistake #4: Flooding your copy with techie talk

When people are prowling the web for a product or service, the last thing they want to have to do is Google words they don't understand. So drowning your audience in triple-point Scrabble words is a surefire way to slash your sales. Folks want to know the benefits of your product or service and how it'll change their lives. And they want to hear that in as few, simple words as possible.

Mistake #5: Using adjectives for evil

I'm not sure when it happened, but frilly, drab adjective demons are disguising themselves as copy angels and they're wreaking pure havoc on sales pages and other online content.

Now, don't get me wrong, the right adjective can turn a drab sentence into a fabulous one in 3.2 seconds. Emotional or sensory adjectives like crappy, dazzling and delightful can help your reader picture or feel something – and when you can make 'em feel something, you're much more likely to get 'em to buy something.

Here are a few ways to banish those pesky adjective demons:

- Drop meaningless, drab filler words like market-leading, cutting-edge and best-in-class, nice and bad.

- Use emotional and sensory words that tell stories and paint pictures such as vibrant, silky, rough, and stinky.

- In order to change the meaning of your sentences, cut lazy adjectives that aren't working.

- Now there are certainly a ton of other common copywriting mistakes, but if you're committing any of these "evil" acts, please stop before you destroy your copy for good.

GYBIG Exercise #7: Edit to "Perfection"

Use the 5-point checklist below to edit your sales page. Don't attempt to be a word superhero and fly through your editing all at once. You catch more goofs when you take your time to edit step-by-step.

Would you prefer a downloadable PDF of this checklist? Get it free at www.baab.biz/FREEActionSheets.

5-Point Editing Checklist

Point #1 – Talk to Yourself

Say what, Apryl? I know it sounds crazy, but reading your sales page aloud is an absolute must if you want it to sound like a real conversation. Why? Because when you say it aloud, you'll naturally stumble where the flow is not quite right.

To improve your page, make note of the places where you stumble and go back to refine the flow of that section. It's also a good idea to record yourself reading the sales page so you can play it back and make sure it oozes with personality AND words that sell.

Point #2 – It's All About Emotions

As a teenager, I loved this song called Emotions by a curly-haired, country talking boy band named H-Town. In it, they talked about how emotions can make you cry, make you glad and make you fall in love.

Same thing goes in persuasive writing. If you want a prospect to fall in love with what you're selling, you have to tap into the emotions that will propel them into action. To get people to read what you wrote and take action, you have to appeal to their feelings and desires. Here are 7 top emotions:

1. Greed
2. Fear
3. Vanity
4. Lust
5. Pride

6. Envy
7. Laziness

Now, go back through your sales page and assess what emotions you tapped into and whether they'll appeal to your prospects. If you think the vibe is off, then go back and examine another emotion you could tap into. Once you have done this, then revise your text to fit the new improved emotional tug at your clients' hearts and wallets. For example, if your buyers are afraid of not making enough money in their businesses, you probably want to lead your sales page with reiterating the pain they're experiencing and present your product or service as the "healer."

On the other hand, say your prospect is all about looking good, then you might consider tapping into the vanity emotion by giving them a glimpse into how fantastic they'll look after completing your fitness program. These are powerful emotions and the easiest and most recognizable ones for newbie writers to tap into. But they're not the only emotions to consider when writing to your prospect. There are other, more appealing emotions that you can tap into once you become a more advanced writer. For now, stick with these and remember the golden rule of persuasive writing – always sell to the heart first … not the brain.

Point #3 – Anticipate Objections

Remember when you'd ask your mom for something and she'd already have a "no" waiting on her tongue before you blurted out the full question? You need those same "mommy" superpowers for your sales page.

When you can anticipate your prospect's objection to smacking the buy button, you have a better chance of making the sale. Go back to the list of objections you created in Copy Shot #2 and make sure your sales page addresses most if not all of them.

Point #4 – Dial a Friend

I have my husband read stuff for me sometimes. Not because he's necessarily my ideal client but because his eyes will most likely see things that mine didn't. And that's why you need to dial a friend when it comes to your own persuasive copy.

If you can get a client to review your draft sales page, that's even better. Just be sure she's cool enough not to judge you if there are crazy "unmentionables" in your raw copy.

Point #5 – Don't Be a "Serial Tweaker"

A serial tweaker is a writer who can't bring herself to share her words with the world. You tweak a sentence here. You change a word there. And the next thing you know, a few weeks have passed and you still haven't published your copy. Bad move. Because it's never going to perfect, but if it ain't published, NOBODY can buy. The great thing about writing today versus in the caveman days is we don't write in stone. So publish it. And if you find you're not getting the results you want, go back and change it.

GYBIG Exercise #7: Don't Let Perfection Paralyze You

I know I said to "edit to perfection" in Exercise #6, but don't risk not publishing your page for the sake of perfection. Do your best and hit send. The world is waiting for your genius – so give the people what they want!

YOU DID THAT!

"Success isn't about how much money you make, it's about the difference you make in people's lives." –
Michelle Obama

You did it, BOSS! You wrote your very own sales page and now you are ready to share your sales page with the world, AND better yet, get the moolah you deserve for your brilliant services or products. Now before you hit publish, remember to double-check to make sure your written text looks just as appealing on the web page as it did in your Word doc.

- You may need to chunk paragraphs again to make sure you're not over the 6-line max as a result of design elements.
- Have a lot of white space on the page to increase readability.
- Use brand colors and larger font sizes to highlight what you really want your readers to notice.
- Take your prospect by the virtual hand and guide her through the page with direct and obvious calls to action.

And that's it! Now, I won't say "good luck" because when you have the right tools and know what you're doing, you don't need luck. So I'll just end with this:

Share your genius. Change the world. Be prosperous!

P.S. If you want to send me a note about how much you loved this book or just wanna say "whaddup," you can drop me a note at: abeverly@baab.biz. I answer all emails personally and would love to connect with you.

MEET THE WORD B.O.S.S.

*"Persuasive writing is all about being
BOLD, OUTSPOKEN, SINCERE and presenting yourself like the
SUPERSTAR you were born to be." – Apryl Beverly*

Apryl Beverly, "The Word B.O.S.S.," is a six-figure, award-winning copywriter who has helped solo entrepreneurs, small business owners, CEOs and marketing executives of big profitable brands generate millions in revenue – all by tapping into the power of words. Known for her educated, "tell-it-like-it-is" writing voice, Apryl has broken just about every grammar rule she ever learned and survived the wrath of her English teachers.

She is a graduate of The Ohio State University in Journalism and the University of Phoenix in Masters of Business Administration in Marketing. She's mom to the most amazing kid in the universe and is married to the masterful "money man."

A LIL' EXTRA SOMETHING

"It takes a village to raise up a strong biz baby." – Apryl Beverly

The following people, websites and tools (listed in no particular order) make up my beautiful "village."

Bad Girl Ventures Cleveland – Where Bad Girls Win (www.badgirlventures.com)

When I participated as a finalist in this program, I had no idea what to expect. I soon found out that it's okay to be a "bad girl" because bad girls win BIG!

Media Mavericks Academy, TeeJ Mercer (iWannaBeAMaverick.com)

Chief Maverick TeeJ showers us with insider Hollywood secrets on getting booked on TV and so much more. Her Mavericks are popping up on *Fox and Friends, The Steve Harvey Show* and *The Doctors,* to name a few! I'd need a few pages to tell you how amazing TeeJ is – just know you NEED her in your life!

Black Owned Business Facebook Group, Ahmir Young (egrassrootsbusiness.com)

This group is jam-packed with more than 30,000 beautiful, intelligent and helpful entrepreneurs at all phases of the biz life. It's the most supportive online group I've ever seen!

The Advanced Marketing Institute – Headline Analyzer (www.aminstitute.com/headline/index.htm)

Not sure if your headline is compelling enough? This site is the place to turn. My DIY clients LOVE this tool. Warning: This tool is highly addictive!

Katherine Weir – Ride or Die Word Badass (www.itjusthappens.ca)

This woman has been riding as my editor-in-crime for more than 3 years. You would've never got your hands on all these fantastic persuasive writing tips had it not been for her.

Hammad Abdullah – Design Extraordinaire (hammadabdullah.com)

Tired of the stock photos and cookie-cutter designs? This is the MAN to call. He turned my mumbo jumbo into a mind-blowing visualization. Didn't you see my book cover, dude?

Tiana Patrice – Best-selling Author & Motivational Coach (fifttytwoshadesoffearless.com)

Her book "Fifty Two Shades of Fearless" is a must-read for those looking for inspiration and guidance on taking the next "scary" big step. Her straight talk is just what the doctor ordered.

Audria Richmond – Branding & Marketing Consultant (audriarichmond.com)

Ms. Audria teaches us how to have a smoking-hot brand that brings in the money! She's all about helping entrepreneurs dream BIG and create BIG.

Rev. Jenenne Macklin – The Spirit & Riches Coach (spiritandriches.com)

The Rev is a beautiful woman inside and out and when she shines her light on other women – baby, it is nothing short of a divine transformation! So glad to have her in my life.

Laura Allahverdi – Life Coach and Game Changer (lauraslifecoaching.com)

Laura's sole purpose is to help people see and act on their full potential. She is a graceful, passionate coach who I proudly call my biz buddy!

Pitch Close Upsell Repeat: A Practical Guide to Sales Domination, David Anderson (Amazon.com)

Dave packed his best-selling book with unorthodox, yet highly successful sales strategies.

Lakeisha Singletary – The Digital Profit Strategist (lakeishasingletary.com)

Lakeisha goes hard in everything she does, and I love that about her. She's all about helping entrepreneurs make more money online.

Amber Aziza – Business Coach (www.asquaredcoach.com)

If you've ever been on Periscope, Facebook – anywhere online, you know all about Ms. Amber. She's passionate about helping entrepreneurs succeed. Her motto: "If you can make a dollar, you can make a million."

Grammarly.com – The Site English Teachers Love

I've been known to break quite a few grammar rules. This site puts me back in line when I need a quick check.

Afterword

This book provides a step-by-step process for writing copy that pierces hearts and opens wallets, so you sell more of your awesome products and services. There's a ton of juicy copywriting secrets and helpful hints on these pages. Most copywriters guard this info with their lives – or they'll charge you an arm and a leg for it – but not me!

To help you execute the process, I created several action sheets and related resources available for free at www.baab.biz/FREEActionSheets.

Download these only if you're serious about applying what you I teach you in this book.

I also recommend that you get started right away. Writing copy that pierces hearts and opens wallets is a learning process. The sooner you begin, the faster you'll develop your skills and the more sales you'll make. I'm here to help. Please share your ideas, feedback and questions by emailing me at abeverly@baab.biz.

I invite you to visit my digi-home at www.baab.biz and check me out on social media at:

    Facebook: https://www.facebook.com/BAABWriting/
    Periscope: https://www.periscope.tv/baabwriting
    Twitter: https://twitter.com/baabwriting
    LinkedIn: https://www.linkedin.com/in/aprylbeverly

Your new clients are waiting. Go get them.

Made in the USA
Lexington, KY
12 December 2017